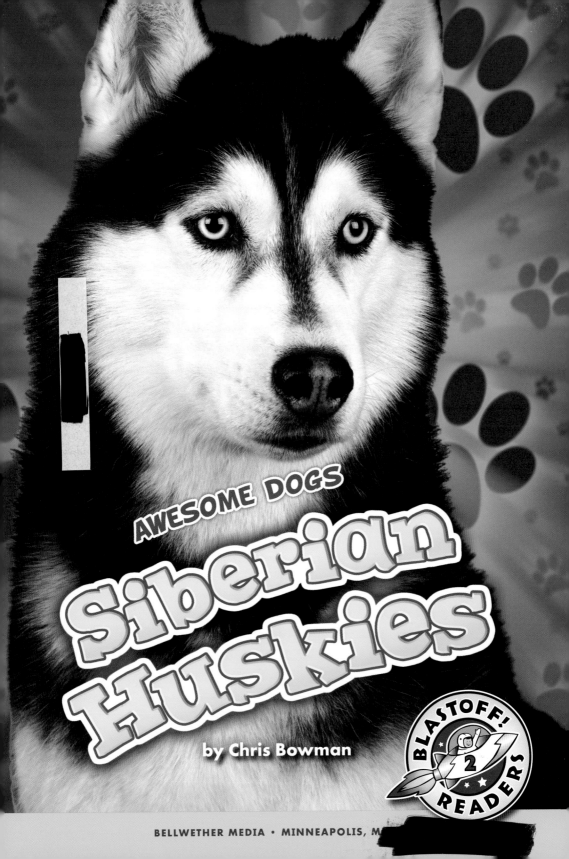

AWESOME DOGS

Siberian Huskies

by Chris Bowman

BLASTOFF! READERS
2

BELLWETHER MEDIA • MINNEAPOLIS, M

Note to Librarians, Teachers, and Parents:

Blastoff! Readers are carefully developed by literacy experts and combine standards-based content with developmentally appropriate text.

Level 1 provides the most support through repetition of high-frequency words, light text, predictable sentence patterns, and strong visual support.

Level 2 offers early readers a bit more challenge through varied simple sentences, increased text load, and less repetition of high-frequency words.

Level 3 advances early-fluent readers toward fluency through increased text and concept load, less reliance on visuals, longer sentences, and more literary language.

Level 4 builds reading stamina by providing more text per page, increased use of punctuation, greater variation in sentence patterns, and increasingly challenging vocabulary.

Level 5 encourages children to move from "learning to read" to "reading to learn" by providing even more text, varied writing styles, and less familiar topics.

Whichever book is right for your reader, Blastoff! Readers are the perfect books to build confidence and encourage a love of reading that will last a lifetime!

This edition first published in 2016 by Bellwether Media, Inc.

No part of this publication may be reproduced in whole or in part without written permission of the publisher. For information regarding permission, write to Bellwether Media, Inc., Attention: Permissions Department, 5357 Penn Avenue South, Minneapolis, MN 55419.

Library of Congress Cataloging-in-Publication Data
Bowman, Chris, 1990– author.
  Siberian Huskies / by Chris Bowman.
    pages cm. – (Blastoff! Readers. Awesome Dogs)
  Summary: "Relevant images match informative text in this introduction to Siberian huskies. Intended for students in kindergarten through third grade"– Provided by publisher.
  Audience: Ages 5-8.
  Audience: K to grade 3.
  Includes bibliographical references and index.
  ISBN 978-1-62617-308-8 (hardcover : alk. paper)
  1. Siberian husky–Juvenile literature. 2. Dog breeds–Juvenile literature. I. Title. II. Series: Blastoff! Readers. 2, Awesome Dogs.
  SF429.S65B69 2016
  636.73–dc23
                          2015031573

Printed in the United States of America, North Mankato, MN.

Table of Contents

What Are Siberian Huskies?

Siberian huskies are calm and happy dogs. They are often called huskies for short.

This medium-sized **breed** likes cold weather.

5

Huskies look friendly.
Their ears stick up.

They have brown or blue eyes.
Some have one of each!

Siberian huskies have double **coats**. Thick **undercoats** keep them warm during winter.

Their outer fur is medium length.
They **shed** often.

Their fur is usually white with gray, black, or red coloring. Some have **agouti** or **sable** coloring.

Siberian Husky Coats

gray   black   red

sable

Many have **masks** across their faces.

Thousands of years ago, the Chukchi people of Siberia first **bred** Siberian huskies.

Siberia

They needed to carry meat home
from hunting. They used huskies
to pull their sleds.

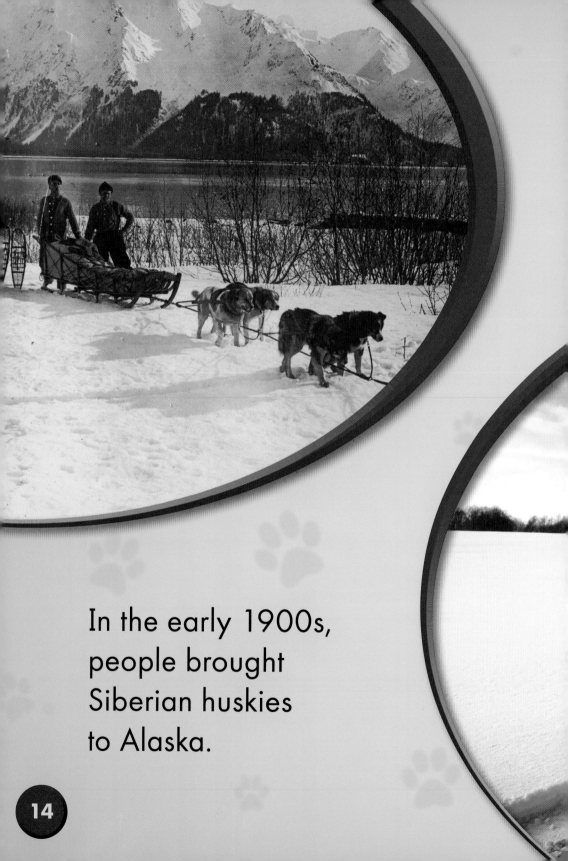

In the early 1900s,
people brought
Siberian huskies
to Alaska.

The dogs became known for running. They won many sled dog races.

In 1925, teams of huskies saved lives. They delivered medicine to people in Nome, Alaska.

Siberian Husky Profile

triangle-shaped ears —

thick double coat

bushy tail

Life Span: 12 to 14 years

Trainability:

| 1 | 2 | 3 | 4 | 5 | 6 |

Hardest to train   Easiest to train

Today, Siberian huskies are placed in the **Working Group** by the **American Kennel Club**.

These **athletic** dogs love to run long distances. This helps them perform special jobs.

Many Siberian huskies are sled dogs. Some work in **search and rescue**.

These friendly dogs like to be in **packs**. Huskies are playful with children and other pets.

They do well in big families!

Glossary

agouti—a coat coloring in which hairs have lines of dark and light colors; agouti is also called the wild pattern.

American Kennel Club—an organization that keeps track of dog breeds in the United States

athletic—being strong, fit, and active

bred—purposely mated two dogs to make puppies with certain qualities

breed—a type of dog

coats—the hair or fur covering some animals

masks—patterns of color around the eyes of some Siberian huskies

packs—groups that live together

sable—a coat coloring that is reddish with black tips

search and rescue—teams that look for and help people in danger

shed—to lose hair or fur

undercoats—layers of short, soft hair or fur that keep some dog breeds warm

Working Group—a group of dog breeds that have a history of performing jobs for people

To Learn More

AT THE LIBRARY
Blake, Kevin. *Balto's Story.* New York, N.Y.: Bearport Publishing, 2015.

Gill, Shelley. *Alaska's Dog Heroes: True Stories of Remarkable Canines.* Seattle, Wash.: Sasquatch Books, 2014.

Johnson, Jinny. *Siberian Husky.* Mankato, Minn.: Smart Apple Media, 2015.

ON THE WEB
Learning more about Siberian huskies is as easy as 1, 2, 3.

1. Go to www.factsurfer.com.

2. Enter "Siberian huskies" into the search box.

3. Click the "Surf" button and you will see a list of related web sites.

With factsurfer.com, finding more information is just a click away.

Index

The images in this book are reproduced through the courtesy of: Adya, front cover; gillmar, pp. 4, 9 (right), 15; Rosa Jay, p. 5; Eric Isselee, pp. 6, 17; Rita Kochmarjova, p. 7; otsphoto, p. 8; joloei, p. 9 (left); Jagodka, p. 10 (left, right); Nataliia Sdobnikova, p. 10 (middle); Dm_Cherry, p. 11; Susan Schmitz, p. 12; SOTK2011/ Alamy, p. 13; Library of Congress, p. 14; Alaska Stock/ Design Pics/ SuperStock, p. 16; Sbolotova, p. 18; Adrenalinapura, p. 19; CebotariN, p. 20; Pavel L Photo and Video, p. 21.